The activities

- The activities in this book are designed to show whether your children are 'ready' to read or are ready for a more difficult reading level. Their wish to read is the best sign of readiness.

- Many skills are involved, but most of them will be mastered unconsciously, just as your children learned to talk without direct teaching. They do not have to be equally good at, for instance, seeing letters distinctly, drawing, copying or telling a story. Success in particular activities should help you to find their strong points.

- The chart on page 32 details some of the skills and the ways these are linked with progress in learning to read.

The stories at Level 1

- There are very few words in these stories; the meaning lies as much in the pictures as in the text. The simple text and pictures will gradually introduce the characters who live in West Street. Your children will probably remember the words very quickly, although they will not be sounding them out letter by letter. This is fine: recognising and remembering words are very important skills in early reading.

- Before you start reading with your children, read the story and activities first yourself, so that you become familiar with the text and the best way to give it expression and emphasis when reading it aloud.

- Alw child boo

- Rea sou comments on the story and the pictures if you wish. Encourage your child to participate actively in the reading, to turn over the pages and to become involved in the story and characters. Even though children can't read, they enjoy guessing what is going to happen from the pictures, and talking about the emotions of the story.

- This may be enough for one sitting, but don't give your child the idea that the book is finished with. Encourage your child to take the book away and to look through it alone, to find any bits that either of you particularly enjoyed.

- Next time you look at the book with your child, suggest "Let's read the story together. You join in with me." The text in the speech bubbles is often the same as the text at the bottom of the page, so one of you can read the text in the bubbles, and one can read the text at the bottom of the page. This time follow the words with your finger under them as you read. Don't stop to repeat words; keep the interest up and the story line flowing along.

- Now ask your child, "Do you want to read the story to me this time?" If your child would like to do this, join in where necessary if help is needed. The timing of this stage will depend on your child's readiness to take over. Do not rush! Try to avoid the idea that

1

reading is a great race where you are always urging children on to harder and harder text.

The activities at Level 1

- The activities at the back of the book need not be completed at once. They are not a test, but will help your child to remember the words and stories and to develop further skills required for becoming a fluent reader.

The activities are often divided into three parts.

- One part is designed to encourage you both to talk about the stories, to predict what will happen and to recall the main events of the story.

- One part encourages children to look back through the book to find general or specific things in the text or the pictures. Your child learns to begin to look at the text itself, and to recognise some individual words and letters. Don't press on with these activities too quickly; your child may need to wait a bit before tackling them. Children's general understanding of a story often comes before their ability to make distinctions between individual words and letters.

- One part suggests drawing or writing activities which will help your children feel they are contributing actively to the story in the book.

- When you and your child have finished all the activities, read the story together again before you move on to another book. Your child should now feel secure with it and enjoy being able to read the story to you.

Read all about it

by Helen Arnold

Illustrated by Tony Kenyon

A Piccolo Original
In association with Macmillan Education

Dad is reading.

Len Maggs
1, West Street
London

Liz is reading.

Sunny Cornflakes

Snap! Crackle! Pop!

Len is writing.

Dear Gran,
Thank you
for my book.
Love from
Len.

Tamla is writing, too.

A big black cat

Tamla's Dad is reading.

How to make your new table

Mrs Rocco is reading, too.

How to make a chocolate cake

Tony is reading.

Daring Dennis

17

Anna is reading.

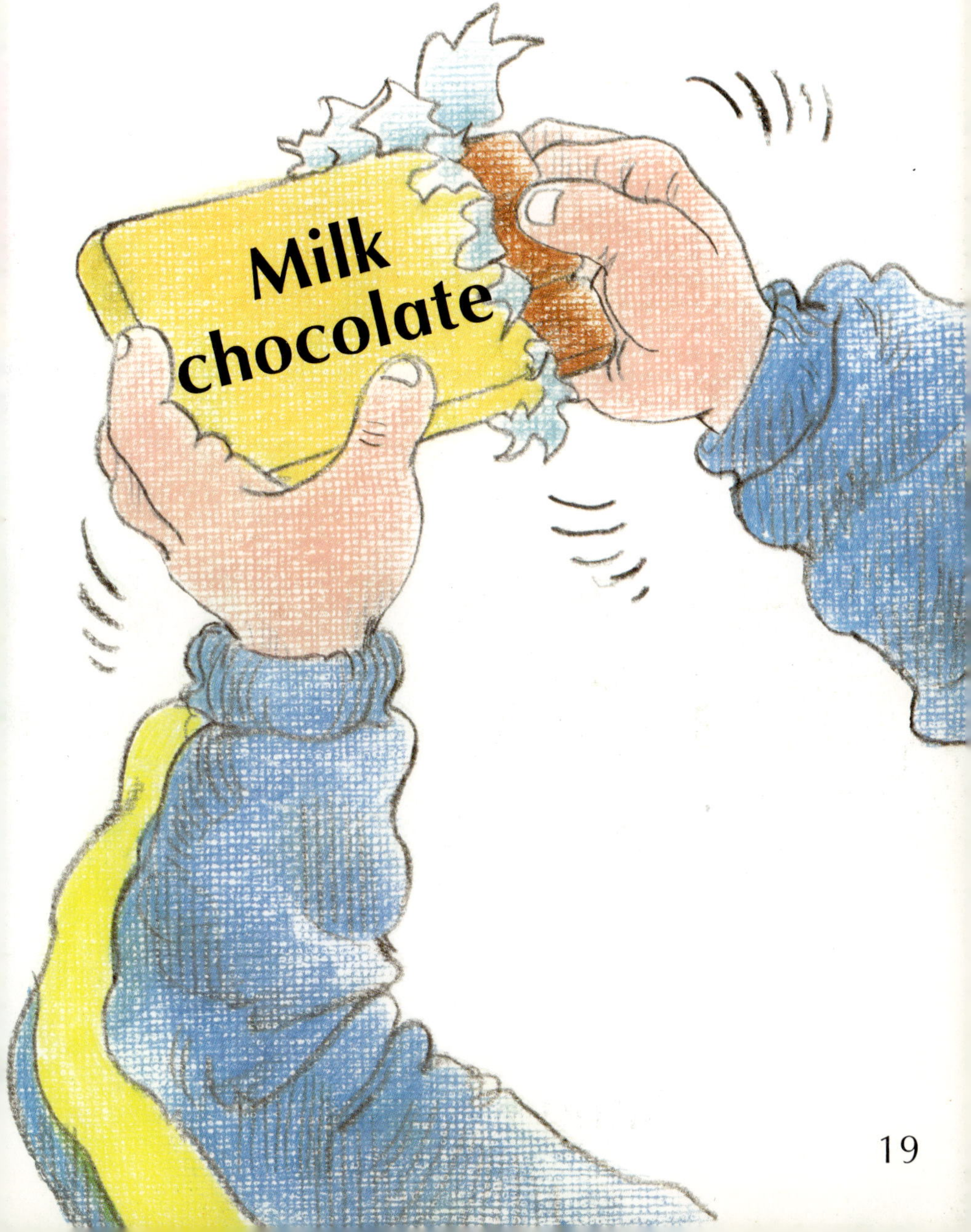
Milk
chocolate

"Where's my chocolate?"

Ben can't read, but he likes eating.

Tops can't read, but he likes eating, too.

Papa is reading.

Ben wins game

They all like reading stories.

Cinderella

Once upon a time

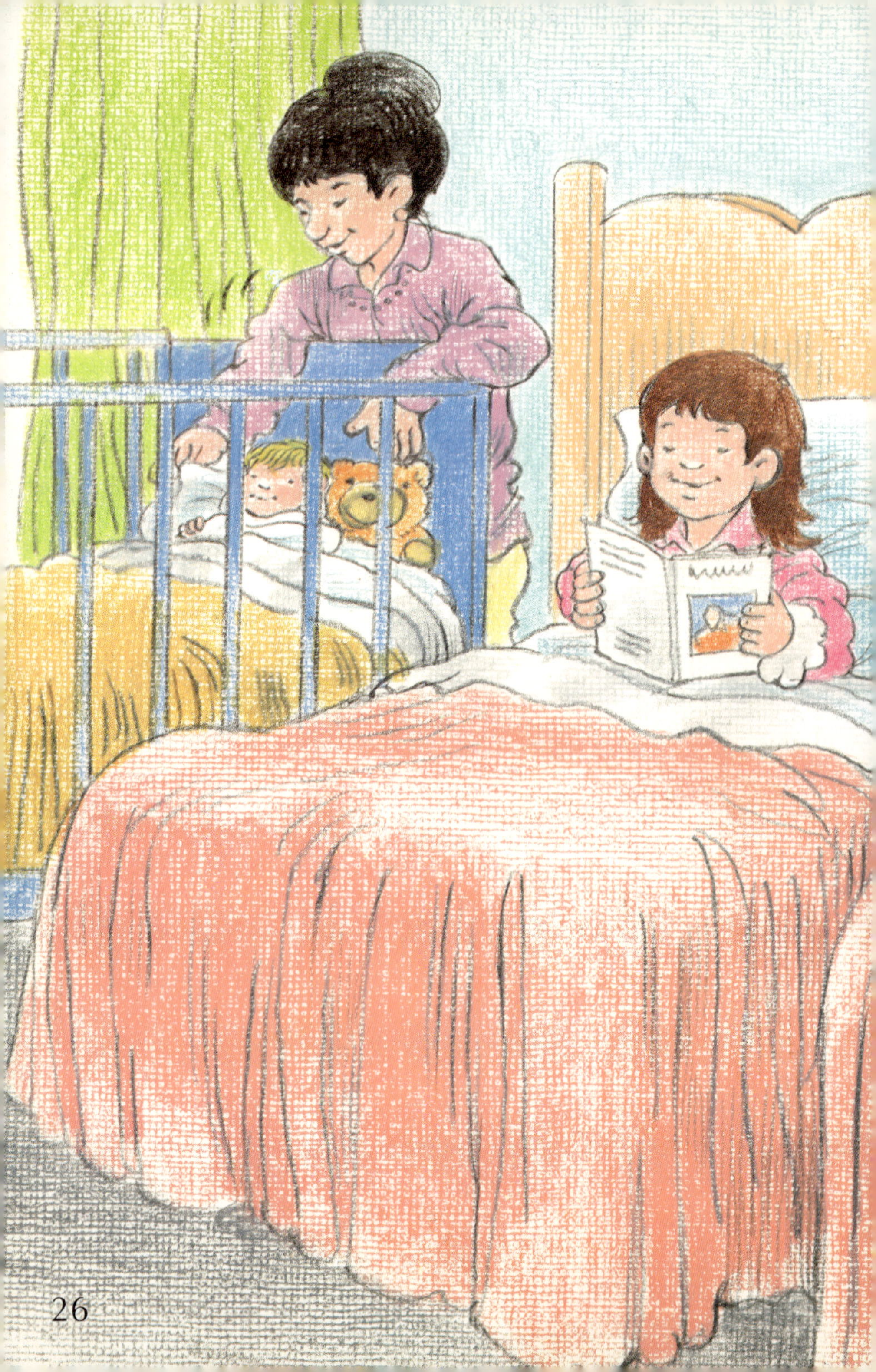

Tops likes stories, too.

Things to talk about with your children

1. Do you know how many houses there are in West Street?
   Can you count them?

2. Who lives in each house? I'll read the names and you point to the door of the house.
   Mr Maggs, Liz, Len and Dennis the dog live in Number 1.
   Mr and Mrs Singh and Tamla live in Number 2.
   Number 3 is empty.
   Mr and Mrs Rocco, Tony, Anna, Baby Ben and Tops the dog live in Number 4.

Looking at pictures and words with your children

1. Can you find the page where Tamla is writing?
   Can you point to what she has written?
   Do you know what it says?

   Who was reading a comic?
   Can you find the page?
   Can you read the name of the story in the comic?

   Who did Len write to?
   Can you find his letter?
   Can you read it?

2. Can you remember the names of all the people in the story who are reading something? I'll write their names down as you tell them to me.
   Let's check the story to make sure you have remembered them all.

3. Can you count all the times the word **reading** comes in the story?

4. Can you find the page where Anna was naughty?
   What did Tony say? Can you show me the words?

Things for your child to do

1. Can you match the pictures with the words? Point to a picture then point to the word.

chocolate

milk

cornflakes

29

2. Write the names of the people in the story onto cards:

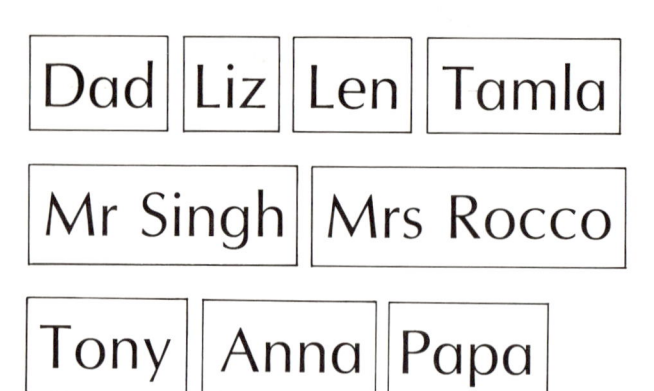

| Dad | Liz | Len | Tamla |

| Mr Singh | Mrs Rocco |

| Tony | Anna | Papa |

Spread the cards out on the table. Ask your child to choose a card and read the name on it (help if necessary).

Can you match the name of the person to one of these pictures?

3. Make a chart as follows:

Reading	Writing

Who was reading and who was writing? Let's put each name card in one of the columns of our chart to show what each person was doing.

4. Can you tell me what the missing words are? I'll read and when I stop, you tell me what the missing word is.

Len Maggs,
1, _____ Street,
London.

Mrs Rocco was making a _____ cake.

Tamla had drawn a picture of a big black _____ .

Len wrote a letter to his _____ .

Tamla's Dad was making a _____ .

31

These activities and skills:	will help your children to:
Looking and remembering	hold a story in their heads, retell it in their own words.
Listening, being able to tell the difference between sounds	remember sounds in words and link spoken words with the words they see in print.
Naming things and using different words to explain or retell events	recognise different words in print, build their vocabulary and guess at the meaning of words.
Matching, seeing patterns, similarities and differences	recognise letters, see patterns within words, use the patterns to read 'new' words and split long words into syllables.
Knowing the grammatical patterns of spoken language	guess the word-order in reading.
Anticipating what is likely to happen next in a story	guess what the next sentence or event is likely to be about.
Colouring, getting control of pencils and pens, copying and spelling	produce their own writing, which will help them to understand the way English is written.
Understanding new experiences by linking them to what they already know	read with understanding and think about what they have read.
Understanding their own feelings and those of others	enjoy and respond to stories and identify with the characters.

First published 1989 by Pan Books Ltd,
Cavaye Place, London SW10 9PG

9 8 7 6 5 4 3 2 1

Editorial consultant: Donna Bailey

© Pan Books Ltd and Macmillan Publishers Ltd 1989. Text © Helen Arnold 1989

British Library Cataloguing in Publication Data
Arnold, Helen
Read all about it.
Level 3
1. English language. Readers — For children
I. Title II. Kenyon, Tony III. Series
428.6
ISBN 0-330-30677-4

Printed in Hong Kong

This book is sold subject to the condition that it shall not, by way of trade or otherwise be lent, re-sold, hired out or otherwise circulated without the publisher's prior consent in any form of binding or cover other than that in which it is published and without a similar condition including this condition being imposed on the subsequent purchaser

Whilst the advice and information in this book are believed to be true and accurate at the time of going to press, neither the author nor the publisher can accept any legal responsibility or liablility for any errors or omissions that may be made